NOTE FROM THE PUBLISHER

Well, it is time for yet another *Ibbetson Street*. We are celebrating our 20th anniversary. That's a long time in the small press world. On the front and back covers of this issue you can view the evocative paintings of Bridget Seley-Galway—a longtime contributor to *Ibbetson Street*.

It has been an active few months for *Ibbetson Street*. Since we last talked, we published a new collection edited by Lee Varon and Marc Goldfinger, *Spare Change News Poems: An Anthology by Homeless People and those Touched by Homelessness.* And the Ibbetson Street Press Young Poet Series (directed by Emily Pineau) has released a new collection of poetry by a talented undergraduate, Daniel Calnan, entitled *To Move a Piano.*

In other news, I presented on a panel for the *Leonard Bernstein Festival* at Brandeis University, where I talked about *Ibbetson Street*'s many grassroots efforts. The panel was headed by Rosie Rosenzweig, who teaches at Brandeis and is part of the Bagel Bards writers group. Also, I was on a panel at the Boston National Poetry Month Festival (cofounded by *Ibbetson Street* poetry editor Harris Gardner and Lainie Senechal) at the Boston Public Library. The panel dealt with creativity and publishing, and, of course, *Ibbetson Street* was part of the discussion.

Another thing that really pleased me was that I was contacted by *EBSCO*, a major scholarly database used by colleges across the country. It seems they want to include as many of the issues of *Ibbetson Street* as they can in a new humanities index they are creating. It should be up in the spring of 2019.

The Endicott College/Ibbetson Street press Visiting Author Series had a good spring. Iraqi War vet Michael Anthony read from his book, *Civilianized: A Young Veteran's Memoir,* and Stephanie Cassalty read from her compelling memoir *Notice of Release: A Daughter's Journey to Forgive her Mother's Killer*

As always, we want to thank Endicott College for their unwavering support. We are especially grateful to Professor Dan Sklar and Dr. Mark Herlihy for all their help over the years. Also, a slap on the back for longtime poetry editor Harris Gardner, designer Steve Glines and managing editor Lawrence Kessenich for another fine issue.

—Doug Holder, June, 2018

Ibbetson Street Press
25 School St.
Somerville, MA 02143

Publisher: Doug Holder
Managing Editors: Lawrence Kessenich, Emily Pineau
Poetry Editor: Harris Gardner
Consulting Editors: Robert K. Johnson, Dianne Robitaille
Art Consultant: Richard Wilhelm
Design: Steve Glines
Website Manager: Steve Glines
Front and back cover images: Bridget Seley-Galway.

Boston Area Small Press and Poetry Scene http://dougholder.blogspot.com
Doug Holder's CV: http://dougholderresume.blogspot.com
Ibbetson Street Press http://ibbetsonpress.com
ISCS PRESS http://www.iscspress.com
Ibbetson Street Press Online Bookstore http://www.tinyurl.com/3x6rgv3

The Ibbetson Street Press is supported by and formally affiliated with Endicott College, Beverly, Massachusetts. http://www.endicott.edu

No simultaneous submissions; no poems previously published in print or online. All submissions must be sent by email only to tapestryofvoices@yahoo.com—as an attachment or pasted into the body of the email.

Advertise with the Boston Area Small Press and Poetry Scene! http://tinyurl.com/ddjcal

CONTENTS

EYEBROWS

I used to pluck an arch into them
and be done, as instructed by the pundits

of my time, and this served me well.
But now the style is straight across,

geometric, triangular, stylized and dark
or something called ombré, requiring

skills, products, and minutes I do not have.
Suddenly I'm wrong-footed as a flapper

penciling in her two thin swoops.
It's fine for me, I'm almost past the demands

of fashion, my magazines have folded,
and beauty preys on the young and radiant.

But every day my young and radiant daughter
struggles with her tools in the mirror,

constructing her brows as she is advised to,
even as she builds the revolution.

—*Laura Cherry*

FEAR STREET

I lived on Main Street in a quiet city,
where the citizens spoke kindly
of those they didn't have to live with,
a liberal city, but underneath
every complacent surface is a set of fangs,
sharp and growing sharper. Hungry
and growing irritable. Fear making it
insatiable. How suddenly it seemed to
draw back its lips. I was surprised.
I said I didn't see it coming.
They said that's because you didn't
have to. It wasn't gnawing on you.
How indignant I was on their behalf.
How I loved my indignation and righteousness.
They rolled their eyes at my innocence
which was expensive and costing
their lives. But I'd never hurt you,
I said. We all live on Fear Street,
they replied, but you couldn't read
the sign. We're all being swallowed
Go ahead, if you don't believe us,
walk into its maw.

—Kathleen Aguero

AN "UKSHEN" IN YIDDISH

An "ukshen" my mother used to say
is the sort of person that even
if you slice them up in little pieces
each piece keeps saying the same thing
a rag falls off the craziness of my heart

and I see myself persistent stubbornly
trying to balance my off-center life
wondering what will deliver me
from the chaos of small control
I look but can't find the word "ukshen"

anywhere only Yiddish fragments
echoing bits of memory which almost
makes sense considering no one
knows what I'm like understands
I'm an "ukshen" except my mother.

—Nina Rubinstein Alonso

OTHER ELEMENTS

The stream's skin of ice
thins. Sunlight tips a trout's scales,
weighs my heart. Spring soon.

A cloud-penned peahen,
so the sun seemed. Then the cock
raised its rainbow tail.

Spring's balmy breezes
stir birds and bees. Wings flutter
like a shed chemise.

Wind parts a poppy's
scarlet skirts of watered silk—
smudge of pubic ash.

The sun's a happy
waitress named Rose, today's sky
a blue plate special.

Sun limns a cloud's rim
in tungsten arcs as other
elements darken.

When light passes through
a prism, something's set free,
something imprisoned.

Dew-drunk crickets jaw.
Frogs mouth gnats. Cicadas gnaw
night's chewy nougat.

The miser moon banks
sunlight, grudges us its change.
Spend your night wisely.

Porpoise backs ruckle
the Sound's glass sheen. Spent breath
slowly sweeps it clean.

Ducks quack, smack butcher's
wax beaks, shed head feathers lustrous
as houseflies' backs.

Thrilled by visitors,
wasps spill like crisp drops of blood

from a paper heart.

Compost thick skins, scraps,
leavings. Blend a dark, rich chaw.
Amend your sick soil.

—*John Canaday*

ICE AFTER A STORM

envelops everything,
brittle glass—

slender, slick branches
interlaced laid
across white air,
a silver-black abstract

bred together
they know their own rattling,
chattering like magpies…

I shudder
in chill crusty morning,
awed by the cold fist of sun

and how small I am
standing here
under the great loud trees

like a child in a circus crowd,
the wild universe
whirling around me.

—*Ruth Chad*

THE EFFECTS OF WATER

The shell, my mother:
>   open, shining,
>   dark indigo underneath,
>   brittle.

The wave, my father:
>   monstrous,
>   appealing,
>   crushing the boats.

The glazed cup, my job:
>   tea-stained,
>   slipping from my fingers,
>   glistening shards.

The beach glass, my dead friend:
>   worn away,
>   only one
>   of thousands.

>   —*Susan Lloyd McGarry*

SANCTUARY

Warm, dark before there was light,
and beating, like wings, all around:
first safe place—her womb.

High vaulted space, two-story windows
that throw beams of red and blue
on the lonely kneeling girl.

You've traveled too far, on treacherous roads
to be jailed or sent back now.
Come, sister stranger: rest a while.

>   —*Gayle Roby*

HOW GOD SPEAKS

I am the chestnut
with leaves like hands. I
am the reaching branches.
Come. Don't you
already know me?
The lapped bark. Rootsap rising.
The pale green shell
with its perfect horns.
I am the hard
dark satin heart
that hurtles toward you.

>   —*Jessie Brown*

DREAMS OF LOVE

I

I am at a party. I am young,
I am learning, I know nothing,
but I arrange her brown hair
in an unusual way—with spirals
scattered through it. It is
done with care. Everyone
turns, everyone stares.
Everyone says what lovely
hair, what a beautiful girl.
It is a simple act of love
that everyone understands.

II

After the party, I can't bear it.
Her lips have touched the glass I
hold in my hand, a simple
highball glass with a trace
of lip balm on the rim—no
lipstick, hers the kind of beauty
makeup only obscures. I fill
her glass with water, put my lips
where hers have been, taste the balm
I tasted when surprising her
with a quick kiss at the door.
I drink deeply.

>   —*Lawrence Kessenich*

EMAIL AT 2AM

No You to hold me or talk to me,
so as the childhood saying goes
"I think I'll go eat worms." Would like
to get more sleep before the marathon miles
today. Do peanut butter filled pretzels
and candied nuts cure cancer? If daughter
saw me just glance at anything
it went in the cart. The freezer's full too,
vegetable muffins, frozen quiche et al.
At least I don't have to cook for
the appetite I don't have. Today
after radiation, I stop off at Southampton MD
for an hour and a half infusion to try
and pump me up. I'm tired of feeling like
a smiley face balloon on a string. If that
doesn't work maybe I should consider the pretzels.
My rambling mind slips into the daily
homespun miracles all around us—
in the sky, the grass, or the look in a bird's eye
or voices all around us. Love, whatever tree
you sleep under at night, I want to go there too.

—*Jo Carney*

QUIET DESPERATION

          The hour of quiet desperation is upon us.
She almost trusts it, alone with only her thoughts,
yearning for something just beyond her reach.

The hour of quiet desperation descends
and she welcomes it in like an old friend.
No use fighting it, she knows who will win.

"Pull up a chair, have some wine,
 I promise to behave, I won't shed a tear.
 I will wait patiently for you to be on your way."

She removes the nightgown from the hook, the garment
so thin you really have to look to see
the roses as she pulls it over her head one more time.

—*Rona Laban*

NEITHER EARLY NOR LATE

You're walking along a road that climbs
past a farm, a field, another farm.

No cars or trucks in driveways; nobody's home
so you can pick which house you want,

this one, a patch of Queen Anne's lace
and two off-white horses in the yard,

broad of back, but plowless, wagonless.
A tabby cat steps by you into the long grass.

You open your mouth to eavesdrop on the leaves
in the wind's throat, their dry fricatives.

Will a dog appear, barking for all he's worth?
Don't listen if he does. Don't forget you are

prodigal and zealot, lookout, wayfarer,
betting all you have on what might happen next.

—*Jennifer Barber*

WEEKDAY MORNINGS

We had a copper kettle that nobody ever shined.
My father filled it to the brim on cold winter mornings.
His egg at the bottom, kettle boiled, egg cooked,
he made the tea and our mother's toast.

After the breakfast there was plenty of water left,
enough to wash and shave at the kitchen sink.
I see him now, in his vest, braces loose
shaving by a round mirror, his face white with soap,

unaware of the cold, or us as we sat alongside
eating porridge, the dog under the table, hopeful.
Our mother having her tea and toast in bed,
she hated the smell of eggs.

—*Triona McMorrow*

HIGH-WIRE

The dying are such acrobats.
-Deborah Diggs

When my mother joined the circus,
she played slide-piano under the Big Top,
learned tumbling from the Spanish family,

could roll and roll as if forever.
Lunchtime we'd marvel
at the Fire Eaters, and Tattoo Man

would muscle the crescent moon for me,
Then she'd practice swinging
on the trapeze. Sometimes

I'd dance beneath her on the sawdust,
or have to climb up partway, talk her
down. She was not quite fit for balance.

I could see that. Once I heard
the Bare Back Rider say,
the Fat Lady ought to stay on the ground.

Nights, in our car on the circus train,
I'd wash her feet for her, rub them dry.
I wasn't happy. I wasn't really sad;

relieved, I guess, or shy to be that close
to my mother. In our bed, I'd wall
my pillow between us—listen

to the horses sway like spun gold!
I had to learn to fend the lions off,
had to learn to love them.

—*Barbara Helfgott Hyett*

AT THE LAKE IN MAINE

While loons croon
their mellifluous lullaby

beneath the beguiling susurrations
of innumerable stars,

fireflies flicker
in the overgrown garden

illuminating the ethereal insouciance
of the angels

who fall silently
in our midst
like diaphanous dreams

—*Ed Meek*

WATER FALLS

As stubborn as rock can be,
it bows to falling water.
Lichens embrace the temporal
minerals and dream of
yesterday's sunburst of sex.
And a brook trout's rheotaxis
is its prayer of thanks
to the gods of evolution.
It's easier for water.
The ocean always beckons.
And what else can water
do but fall?

—*Gary Metras*

HALF FULL

Yahrzeit glass, half-depleted,
Replenished with memories,
The not-forgotten but less bereft,
Mortality's debris noted by its absence.

Living flame, a slow dance,
No breath, no breeze,
Perhaps a presence,
Transitory visitor,
Or one who never left,
The journey not completed.

—*Harris Gardner*

DEEP IN THE JOURNEY

After decades of brief
but always lively chats
at noisy family gatherings,
I happen to be alone with you

where you lie in a hospital bed,
your drugged eyes barely open.
And—surprised

       by a surge of sadness—
I see the two of us, aged and grey,
clinging to a lifeboat
overturned near a shore

that only I will be able to reach.
How can it be we were never more
than mere acquaintances?

—*Robert K. Johnson*

LAUTREC'S DIARY: ENTRY #2

Dancing at the Moulin Rouge
Montmartre, October 1890

It was her stockings. They first trembled
the chalk in my hand. How they flared
red as twin tongues clappering guttural
French under the brown bell of her dress:
So gauze thin a cicada's wing—
So diaphanous and ungravitied as though lifted
by a ligature of lamplight.

The aristocrat in me wanted her
unstuttered absinthe, her
burnt sugar twirl between bourbon
and burgundy.
                    I know it should
not have been captured—that some phenomena
are meant to be as ephemeral as mayflies—
as Robespierre's ghost glimpsed at Errancis.

                    But I needed to preserve her
for the coming
          century. One where all women
would dance as she— where abandon would be
less rehearsed— movement more style than stunt.

Yet, I fear women like her
will always be envied
                         yet, misplaced
for the way men moth toward them like whore-flame.

For how their feet mistress the air.
For the way their limbs beat night
to a bruise of panting shadow.

—*Regie O'Hare Gibson*

IN THE CITY OF PERFECT PITCH

when I staggered forward
my steps swirled around me like cutting edges
like fluid curves from nowhere, groaned
down to my feet from their orbit, the unknown
they seeped into the breaking of myself

imperfect steps

when I lost the word
my voice hid, spiraling the hurts like heavy spells
like trapped-ghosts from the darkest corners, floated
crowning the in between silences from past karma

imperfect sounds

when my mother, would carry me to the heights of Tagore and Palacios
where pearled dreams could be gazed upon, their ripples
hanging me from enmeshed ropes
like a crucifixion of my myths

imperfect dreams

when my father slipped from our lives
where the absent-presence of his once caring form vanished
his arms unfolded like Christ
an open blister   renewal of needed blood
rusted the edges of knives: the magic three

my perfect life   his imperfect absence

in the city   perfect pitch

.

—*Beatriz Alba del Rio*

MERMAIDS IN MOONLIGHT

This day the ocean has a conversation with the shore.
The rocks call out to the sea, "Amuse us, dance for us."
The ocean in all its glorious fluidity is not shy,
surf leaps; waves roll and pirouette to land.

Even when the dunes sleep, the ocean does not stop.
It is daring, stormy, blue unbroken,
then eternal chain of wave,
majestic and infinite.

Beach stones dream of mermaids in the moonlight.
Starfish float in glittering twilight waters.
Sand castles stand tall waiting for their owners to return.
Bottled messages are everywhere, singing nature's trance.

Seashells awaken at dawn and open pearly eyes
to see the Sun God's face upon the earth.
This day the ocean has a conversation with the shore
and all of the blue planet is alive, as it listens and awaits.

—Louisa Clerici

FLOATING IN BLACK WATER AMONG THE STARS

On summer mornings when I kicked and stroked the lake
water filled my mouth, blue lips & choking. I stood
shivering up to my bony knees. I do not want
to deadman float on a summer day with teeth chattering and goose flesh. The teacher's voice
shouting *relax* does not cease my quivering.
It will take 20 years
and a dive into Gloucester Harbor in my backyard
to emerge amid salt froth with my breath
flowing in and out   easily
into a Cape Ann night
so fear   vanishes
and time   nearly
stops. Here.
I am.
The stars   over my head
swimming.

—Branton Shearer

SUMMER'S DUSK TO CITY NIGHT

The air's cooled blanket
waves over my skin with the breeze.
I look up to the leaves quiver in response,
and higher still to the bright half Moon
peeking through gray blue to waning light—
as it expands down,
to disappear behind a mix of architecture,
where the sun has since set.

An hour ago everything was different,
when the light was glaring before the end of day.

Now I turn to the Moon reflected in a blackened window,
creating another curtain to peek through.
Now the night couples city lights,
from shops, strangers' windows, and cars passing;
soften the landscape of brick and cement.
Now my imagination expands into endless stories,
separate from mine, beyond my before.

—Bridget Seley-Galway

6

--after a painting by Samuel Bak

The tablets of the Law are twin sarcophagi. In one rests I-Am-The-Lord, hands folded, eyelids closed in practiced indifference, Mother and Father dolls nested by his side, Sabbath kitten curled at his feet. In the other, the restive Thou-Shalt-Nots clamber over each other to claim a spot to lie down. But 6, 6, once so fat and sure of himself, rolling at will over the countryside, what shall they do with him, swabbing the floor with his tunic, filling the hall with his *No No No*.

—Lee Sharkey

HOMAGE TO GINSBERG

"I have seen the best minds of my generation"
dive into clouds of simulacra –
numbers, models, algorithms, formulas –
and I have heard too many throats
howl at the emptiness of galaxies.

In the meat departments of supermarkets
I have seen too many boys casting glances needlessly furtive
at well-fed butchers and aproned clerks,
too many girls fumbling in the dark with alien erections
and in daylight with astonished pregnancies.

I have seen too many fine minds in my era
swear the Hippocratic Oath
and, with hyperkinetic faith,
strive, and strive, for years,
before greed and bitterness both
turn the Hippocratic into the hypocritical,
before, crazed by bureaucratic metrics,
atheism eats them alive.

The coarsest minds rise to the surface
like gasoline on water and, lit up by power,
burn with raw, elemental energy.
Other minds tell the story of Moloch,
in the ancient world god of child sacrifice
by fire; in Milton's, ungod, ally of Satan;
in ours, a monster run amok.

—Llyn Clague

INTENSITIES IN TEN CITIES

1.

Ordered a Manhattan in Manhattan,
in an act of adolescent irony.
Tall buildings with trash at their feet
evoked giant oaks in October.
After, Pennsylvania Station rocked
like a small boat on a big sea.
A striking trash collector
blamed "the City" for the strike.
Noncommittal, I waited for the train.
By the time it came, I was in a shell.

2.

Visited the Liberty Bell in Philly,
surprised it was so small.
Its size is the perfect metaphor
for our dwindling civil rights.
Independence Hall was badly in need
of regular maintenance.
Philly is old & I felt & saw it
from a city bus that ran the length
of the city where liberty was born
& where brotherly love is an ideal.

3.

In Atlanta the strip clubs
are popular destinations
for home-boys & tourists alike.
Girls will sit, nude, at your tiny table.
A generous tip & an expensive drink
will get you some Southern hospitality.
They come from all over the South
to dance around naked for money.
I asked them, why Atlanta?
"Most modern city in the South," they replied.

4.

Minneapolis in the wintertime
reminded me that climate
defines each human environment.
Equipped with temperature-controlled walkways
you can shop for Viking souvenirs all day
& never go out in the cold.
Across the frozen river
St. Paul is the shy twin.
The parking ramps have battery chargers

to save time & defeat deep freezes.

5.
Detroit streets felt tense
like an engine wound to the max.
People avoid your glance
or challenge you with a steely stare.
The Renaissance Center needs a renaissance.
Empty spaces outnumber full ones.
Whole neighborhoods of abandoned homes
look like apocalyptic kindling.
At the Greyhound Bus terminal
many of the riders look terminal.

6.
The tall spires of Churchill Downs
stand guard over the main gate
where thousands pour in
to watch a two minute race.
Later in downtown St. Louis,
a bar leaked strains of the *St. Louie Blues*.
I thought of W. C. Handy, Louie Armstrong &
the great Chuck Berry, father of rock & roll.
At the museum I couldn't get
Johnny B. Goode out of my head.

7.
Chicago, the 1968 Democratic Convention:
riot police rioted, blooding the ones
they were paid to protect.
Many sweetheart deals were made & kept.
One honest man stood out from the rest,
but they beat him too.
We escaped the cops but
we were almost murdered
by some drunken local teens with tire-irons
who hated us & everything we stood for.

8.
In Toronto the college students
truly loved American movies.
We saw a forgettable one, but
the crowd cheered its loud approval.
The streets were clean & the people
greeted us with innocent smiles.
Later, we were paranoid
to smoke pot in our hotel,
but we wanted to use it up

before crossing the border back to reality.

9.
Dallas sprawled, brown & dusty.
The smell of barbeque permeated
the dry air. We drove for hours,
but got nowhere under the big sky.
Strong winds blew us around
like tumbleweeds on the run.
Walking around The Galleria,
people smiled & conversed happily.
The big mall has more dimension
than the landscape they live in.

10.
Gettysburg is still fighting the Civil War.
All the restaurants are blue & grey.
Every neighborhood in town
has its own proud battlefield.
There are Civil War souvenir stores
that sell maps to historic scenes of carnage.
They take you through neighborhoods
to big, green lawns where men died young.
Monuments to conflict occupy the streets
like an army of solidified ghosts.

—*Eric Greinke*

COVER THE EARTH

High on the side of a shed where Main Street ended
with a gradual turn to the right at the C & NW tracks
hung the world, a big plywood disk painted green,
with a small but apparently bottomless bucket
of red enamel tipped and pouring over it, the red
running down over all of America, dripping away
from its sides, and as we leaned our bicycles into
the turn up Northwestern Avenue toward the park
with its two miserable bears in their stinky cages,
in big blocky letters it told us to COVER THE EARTH
and we've done just that, and though those bears
died long ago, and though that sign was taken down
so many years ago that few remember it, just now
I leaned into another turn and saw it there.

—*Ted Kooser*

THE BLOODY LANE

"I am poured out like water. . . "
- Unnamed soldier, Antietam, Sept. 17, 1862

At Gettysburg, where ghosts still rise
to fight the war, the minie balls, the shot and shell,
the smoke and noise entombing them, they take again their rest
beneath the trees where they once slumped, their shirts and blouses filled up
with blood, the sharp first sight of nothingness
the light, and yet the days

when crowds have gone, the late sun cools
and bluebirds perch on monuments, they think
of how their wives are gone, and now their children's children gone,
now all together singing hymns, all gathered
by the post and rails, the worm fences that ended it.

Winners, losers then, their souls
were consecrated, their graveyard now a holy place, the spirits
rise again to pray, the sun warming their folded hands.

But Antietam was a killing pen
the Sunken Road a slaughter pit
where Union troops, their heads lowered
charged blindly into Rebel fire that lifted them right off their feet
and slammed them to the ground again, their corpses
piled five men deep, their heads turned white,
their souls to ash and those

who fought can't rest
can't rise to find their families, the Bloody Lane
still rolls over their barreled hands,
their stolen lives.

—*Susan Demarest*

AN ORDINARY DAY

Pray for a shining that may well happen,
Either aura rising to merge with sky
Or hitherto unmemorable blue.
Homer never understood the color
That tinted breathless visions of heaven
And masked the storm-tossing tidal fury.

Not that one should expect all-out fury.
Although, inscrutably, it does happen.
Earth, left behind, abandoned by heaven,
Makes do. Its denizens research the sky,
Build astrologies of lifelong color.
Prospects, perfuse, extend even to blue.

So, still we stand awash in sea-salt blue.
The hours about us bend in closed fury,
Our faces tint free of bloody color
As day gallops by. How does that happen?
Do Apollo's horses, trawling the sky,
Roll up the carpet of quantum heaven?

Sometimes a thought can burst into heaven
Then catch us unaware, when waxing blue.
Silence seems to rule the cathedral sky
At those times, represses the fixed fury,
Interrupts disorder bound to happen.
Here truth totters, halting, without color.

Celebrations of love—Oh what color!
Each minute blessed in a fazed-out heaven,
Multiplying your face. It could happen,
Could fall apart, a blue on deep, deep blue,
A furtive smile before tempest fury.
Vows, like buttresses, hold in place the sky.

Daydreamed history fills the curves of sky,
Our time a blink of eternal color,
Lightning strikes, bolts of yesterday's fury.
Cherubim nurture the buds of heaven
As we paint each other warrior-blue
Waiting for portents of what will happen.

Bright sky, perfect metaphor for heaven,
Music's warmth felt in the color of blue,
Let fury's verses cool. Let love happen.

—Dennis Daly

REVIEW OF IN *PRAISE OF THE USELESS LIFE: A MONK'S MEMOIR*
By Paul Quenon O.C.S.O.
(Ave Marie Press)

After living six decades in the Cistercian (Trappist) Monastery of Gethsemane, Paul Quenon has written a quiet, self-effacing journal of the heart, which periodically breaks out into syllabic dance and grammatical song. This memoir purports to portray the life of an ordinary man living in an unconventional community, a spiritual haven that attracts both simple penitents and intellectual paragons. However, a man, who keens at the death of trees, claims Emily Dickinson as his soul sister, writes exquisite poetry, and engages in a mysticism that he calls "the choreography of heaven" doesn't strike me as ordinary at all.

Throughout this personal chronicle Quenon weaves in scenes from the life of Thomas Merton, as well as reiterating much of Merton's counter-cultural wisdom. It could not be otherwise. Early on Quenon had read Merton's autobiography, The Seven Storey Mountain, and Merton's stature as a modern-day monk had been one of the draws that convinced him to enter the monastery. Once there Merton became his novice master, adding layers of influence onto the young man. Other novices schooled with Quenon during Merton's stint as novice master included a university valedictorian, a lawyer (presumably there for repentance), a missionary back from New Guinea, a psychologist, a later-in-life college president, a soon-to-be brain surgeon and Ernesto Cardenal, who was to emerge as an influential poet and controversial Sandinista revolutionary in Nicaragua.

Quenon knows his audience and relates many inside baseball vignettes about Merton. In one lightly humorous story the young Quenon appears at Merton's door to ask him, "What is the meaning of Zen?" In answer Merton bops Quenon on the head with a book. When Quenon persists in questioning this expert in eastern religion and philosophy, Merton says, "There is a cherry tree outside the window," and leaves it at that.

Mother Nature apparently took over Quenon's education where Merton left off. She provides him with daily, twenty-four hour classrooms, stirs his enzymes, raises his energy, and generally nourishes his soul. Going out into the weather is not only part of his life but also a spirit-lifting ritual. "I am governed and made into something larger than myself," says Quenon. "One morning appears as a Chinese painting," he continues, "with cloaks of fog concealing here, partly there, revealing hills, trees, and fields. Another morn displays a brilliant sprawl of clarity, the color too good to be true, unbearably perfect, until the sun heightens and the sky blanches in the midday heat."

One of the chapter sections in Quenon's book he entitles Eminent Trees I Have Known. Here he voices the affecting kinship he felt upon the demise of two linden trees, killed in order to make room for a new infirmary. He studies his own reaction objectively. "I watched from a distance as they were plowed over with a bulldozer, and the sight provoked my voice to a high, soft pitch," he says. "Such feelings of kinship were a surprise to me; I had never made that sound before, yet it seemed the only decent thing to do at the moment."

Quenon, not only sleeps under the stars most nights, but has molded his meditational life around locations with expansive views and open to the weather. Among these sites is the porch of Merton's old hermitage, about a mile into the woods behind the abbey. Quenon is the caretaker of the hermitage and has escorted many renowned visitors there, including Nobel Prize laureates Seamus Heaney and Czeslaw Milosz. He often sits in a chair with a brass plate attached to the top that says, "Bench of Dreams." It was affixed there by a man who had been assistant secretary general of the United Nations for forty years.

Monks have built-in models for their style of life. I'm thinking of the desert fathers, St. John of the Cross, St. Teresa of Avila, and St. Therese of Lisieux. Although familiar with the aforementioned, Quenon seems to prefer the poet Emily Dickinson as an exemplar of Trappist life and thought. He quotes many of her poetic lines including these,

Growth of Man—like Growth of Nature,
Gravitates within.
Atmosphere, and sun endorse it—
But it stirs—alone.

Each its difficult Ideal
Must achieve—Itself—
Through the solitary prowess
Of a silent life.

My favorite chapter in Quenon's memoir he entitles Battle of Wits with a Mockingbird. It's pretty funny. As the monk tries to sleep outside on the porch of the monastery's lumber shed, a mockingbird begins an unforgettable aria. At first Quenon tries to communicate with the bird like Native Americans were once wont to do, making an oracle out of the creature. Then he begins to yell at the bird. But the bird believes this is a show of positive enthusiasm. Finally, dead tired, the monk begins flapping his blanket, mimicking a bigger bird. This works—for a while. But the next night the bird is back, having figured out the blanket trick. And this epic battle goes on night after night with Quenon using multiple stratagems like setting up a plastic owl decoy to scare the bird or throwing water into the trees. Yet none of these techniques work. Each defeat of monk by mockingbird Quenon memorializes with a haiku, such as,

I wish talent star
with night variety shows
would go off the air.

And this one,

The Mocker, all night
Harasses the neighborhood
—Damn sociopath!

Finally after moving to a new sleeping place the monk planned and carried out a sneak attack, violently shaking the bird's tree. This successfully startled the bird and he absented himself from the vicinity. Now, however, Quenon exhibits all the telltale signs of remorse. He clearly misses the clever show-off, and says so.

Quenon's literary window into the everyday life of Trappist monks is anything but useless. It frames the monastery, and, by extension, humanity as a vital buzzing hive of meaningful encounters, with its hooded denizens conjuring up perpetual moments of unique existence and creative imagination. Beware of this book if you've lost your sense of childish play, if you live a life without song or dance, or if you feel silly communing with trees. It could change you.

—Dennis Daly

THE LINE

I rue the glib scowl of this line I cast,
wishing it less from the head, more from the heart,
maybe giving a joyful skip as it announces

there's nothing in the world it would rather do
than validate my otherness in a sailboat,
the sails and lines snapping alive for able hands.

Yet see how my line and its followers
blur on the fine white nap
of my journal's sacrificial page, the goddamn spray

my nemesis, yet delightful.
If the sea would not mock me, I'd bless these sailors
who let me aboard for the ride alone, and to hell with

so much that's required of this sail and that, and the many
ways you must aim a boat if you've any
sense of the helm, the current, the wave,

the daffy whims of wind and sky.
I, miserable, elated, praise
clear vision and graced response

to the invisible: praise the sailors' leaping about,
grabbing and cleating this line, letting that line loose;
praise their knowing the jib from the mainsail . . .

My Pilot's soft nib is kind to the sodden page.
I'm not very fond of this poem, but the ride
is palpable as a wet ass on a torturous sea

while wind and wave and sunlight blast me with beauty
I'd not have missed for all the anchors
on this grudging craft I ply,

the cold spray, the shore flung away.

—Tomas O'Leary

ON THE EDGE—

the rhythmic chafe of the ocean against the shore,

endlessly alluring, hypnotic—the sea's

might and breadth—its uncharted depths

almost alien, a parallel universe

to the fragile earth we inhabit carelessly—

as if all of life were a renewable commodity,

as if our ascendancy rose above a cosmic moment,

as if bargaining with a pantheon of gods can atone

for our sins and the sins of our fathers, as if we could ride

through eternity on the crest of a breaking wave…

—*Linda M. Fischer*

EAGLETON'S CREDO
"Poetry is a superior form of Babbling."
        -Terry Eagleton, *How to Read a Poem*

Just by existing, Poetry fulfills
our deeply held Utopian desires;
a form of life that's not so much in thrall
to duty, but turns obligation's call
back towards indulgence of our wayward will
to flirt with those unattached signifiers.

Suspend your grim, communicative labors!
Come to the fields of semiotic sport
where sound and meaning recklessly cavort.

Lofty Poetry covets its neighbor's
wife, its slave, its house, its horse and cart;
freed from loveless marriage to one meaning,
Poetry is superior babbling,
convincing us that antic play is Art.

—*Denise Provost*

SHROOMS

Caps of puffballs appear scaled
where darker skin melds with the white.
Puffballs are spongy to the touch
and white meat when they're cut.

How nice to know them,
frying in the buttered pan,
bronzing, ready to please
our tongues.

Or turn to their decked-out sisters,
the morels, so savory.
Back in the day Dean Ford,
with his buzzard's eye,

saw them where I saw not,
and we picked a mess. . . .
Don't let me forget
the magic ones,

way down south near
cow plops. Before
I'd had a chance to nibble
one or two

I was gone,
not so much out of this world
as in it in deeper than I'd known
since I popped out of the womb.

I hadn't known that paradise
wasn't really lost, the trouble
was in our eyes. . . .
What poets try to tell us.

Now, mostly, I buy buttons
from the grocery store. There's
a million ways to slice them up,
sauté, and have your way with them.

Up north, near a mountain home,
there's a pipeline you can follow
into chanterelle promised land.
They're everywhere, and soon

you've filled your plastic bag.

Your little daughter, sleeping
in an upstairs room, sniffs them out,
and down she toddles to join the feast.

—Bert Stern

THE LINE OF ILLUSION

*They say some are born to sorrow
Some to joy.*

Step too far you will fall over graves,
the roots of giant trees,
as whole families picnic with the dead.

Who is the dark-eyed mother, does she dream
in color, of a life rare and true?
Does she wait, not for a prince, but
for the moment
at the end of day as light shifts,
and two might meet.

What if, when a man comes to die
he has not lived?
What can the undertaker tell from
his wrinkled face, from
the no-face of the blown apart?
Did anyone
in his recollection die happy –
knowing all was well that whatever could be done
was done; that broken bits were mended
as best as could be
in the wind and rain and torment?

If a dead branch flowers there might be
a trace of water, and if you stand on the shore,
look to the far hills,
there might be hills, not phantoms.

—Molly Mattfield Bennett

ON THE WAY TO OUR WEDDING

The air is thick with salt, visible. Wet
tires on wet asphalt spin
over and over, halt us
on the tree line. We emerge
from upside down, spun out,
a little blood, windshield opened
to air and debris. I climb through
gasoline and crushed bouquets, roses
and baby's breath. My dress sweeps
glass. Stockings torn. No shoes.

You stand beyond the brimming headlights,
accountable –
Carol.
Carol.
You touch my hand.
Here are your shoes.
I'd trust every force of the world,
if the world would gather us in.
You take my hand. We walk on
like ground fog combing the woods.

—*Carol Hobbs*

AFTER YOU HAVE NEVER LEFT

Driving to the prayer and sacred room
there are those who pass me in white pick-up trucks
and the twilight not yet comes upon us a cool breeze
in summer, a night after recorder in the forest
and the adolescent boy said "beautiful" – a toddler
took my book of poems – "I want that one" with the
photo of the ocean on the cover held to her chest
because my son will be singing in perfect pitch
a prayer for bending, as the trees bend in late
summer light, to kiss the hidden moon
so I have twenty names as I drive, and a
pulse of honey in my heart, say to myself
a line from Isaiah as a motorcycle passes
"The lion and the lamb shall lie down together
and a little child shall lead them" knowing
there are those worms, mere crawling politicians
who would steal the breath of a baby with
a broken heart valve, and the broken wings
of our hawk high above the car as I cruise
with you the hidden, healed in a moment
a kiss that mends the bones broken
in Psalm 34, when David feigned insanity
to save his life – and you have never left

—Judy Katz-Levine

A LIVELINESS

A man on the edge of the sidewalk,
on a low chair, his back to the storefronts,
was playing an accordion.

Crowds wandered by, passing right through
the thick chords, the rhythms,
and crescendos.
If they saw him, it was only for a second.
If they dropped change into the open box at his feet,
it was as they turned away.

He ignored them, rested
in the weary pause between each ending
and each beginning,
before letting his attention be taken again
into that liveliness, apart
from the street and himself—

so there he was, almost invisible among us,
the only one playing an accordion,
and playing for us to listen, for our coins,
as if we weren't there.

—*Hilary Sallick*

THE LAZY LLAMA

The Lazy Llama Cafe blends into a block on the Lower East Side. Two tin bowls, painted with paw prints, depress the Astroturf on the stoop. A few wisps of fur, a few pellets of dog food float on muddy rainwater. A Nike trainer dances a half foot from the two bowls, the hilt of her slender calf sheathed in black LuluLemon, save for a few inches of smooth pale skin. Bounces to the rhythm of Frank Ocean's *Nights* leaking out the scrunched accordion window. A middle aged Haitian man named Daniel sits a few yards away on an old plastic chair whose legs bend under his weight swollen feet spill out of untied sneakers; he lowers his novel to eye for generous passersby. A paper cup adorned with a cartoon Llama lolls beside his foot.

—*Avi Chad-Friedman*

NEW ENGLAND WINTER

He shoveled a space right in front of the house.
It took all morning, back aching, bundled up,
in black gloves in the numbing cold, with more
forecast. Late for his visits — to Children's and

Mrs. Gallagher's and the cop who'd been shot
by a psychopath paroled the week before — he rocked
and rocked till the tires took hold and crunched
into the street, with just enough windshield clear to see.

As soon as he left, a car pulled in with steamy windows,
music loud, to drop off two kids across the street
at the first floor daycare center in the purple house.
Hugs and kisses and mommy's off, a nurse in the ICU

where she sees him, through the small meshed window,
collar up, rubbing and blowing on his cold hands,
while behind her, machines around bed number three
start beeping louder, and with escalating urgency.

—*Richard Hoffman*

THE MAN NEXT DOOR

I try not to ask him what he's got
for himself, mid-life, and balancing
on the spine of obligation
as he reaches into rainbowed
baskets of laundry and groceries,
just inside clouded-over windows.

I imagine how the wrapper of his years
might split into sixteen different meanings,
green under morning's bell.
In the oily kitchen, he pours coffee
as the others head out toward the city.

He listens to stories of shipwrecks
and economies, treasures and wayward birds,
radio voices unperturbed, the comfort
of reportage. Here the future is fearless
and the dog in the living room ready
for a run to the park where the lawns
lift in a dome above the garbage below.

Moving from place to place, every-
where, he must come across himself.
Soon the ones who love him
will return, a quiet gathering.
Days sink like pale silver pins
in a square velvet cushion.

—*Mary Buchinger*

NO ONE TOLD ME

I'd asked the oncologist to call me if my mother was
dying. *We're hopeful,* he'd say. That's how he talked.

So if I despaired, I was letting her down.
If I felt hopeful, I was deluding myself.

I was hurled in the grip. Rip-
tide pulling me out.

Thanksgiving, my stepfather hired a cook. We ate
at my mother's table. Aunt, uncle, cousins.

My mother was stuck in the hospital,
I, too numb and under the thumb

of something huge, unspeakable.
Fear running through the gravy.

My aunt told me she'd try to be a mother to me now.
She ate only a baked potato she mashed with her fork.

At my mother's funeral, when I could have been rending
my clothes, I put on make up, flirted with an old boyfriend.

I was 26. A body must break. I swelled up
just like my mother had. Terrified, I studied

the veins of my hands, the red and blue rivers
ready to burst. An electric fence circled my brain.

When I touch it in my mother-dream,
I bolt awake.

—*Wendy Drexler*

DREAM WITH MY FATHER

"Yes," I say to my father, "yes,
hedges-of lilacs and forsythia."
On waking, I'm sixty-eight years older,
his voice from the dream still sounding,
marveling he would propose this.
I remember he'd told me the forsythia
bloomed early the April I was born.

In the dream the sun warmed our backs,
as we dug up the stuff or our yard—
crockery shards, bits of brick,
tarnished gum wrappers—
shoveling deep hollows for the roots
to withstand the wind and all weathers.
This was Schenectady.

But he was in his own hollow
from which no one could free him,
until mania yanked him out;
his vitriol flung in our faces,
one hand slapping the other,
demanding we witness his rants,
as he chased us from room to room.

Now that I'm grown, and he's safely dead,
I see his volcanic rages
freed him from his pall of despair.
May this fragile compassion take root,
yielding love and my final freedom,
and may the sweet breath of its blossoms
reach him in the underworld.

—*Ann McCrea*

MY OWN PRIVATE OCEAN

'The streets that Balboa walked were his own private
ocean, and Balboa was drowning.' End of story.
—August Wilson

After I OD'd my mama took me to the doctor. I didn't
want to go. It was an accident, I said. Won't happen again.
I know better now. But mama marched me in and that doctor,
he loved to talk. I zoned out to the sound of his voice.

The doctor told my mama part of an addiction
is the thrill of the high. He called it dopamine.
Added incentive is fear of withdrawal. Addicts, he said,
are motivated by both reward and avoidance.

Those are just words, mama. I live in an ocean.
When the tide is high, I rule the waves. But when
that water recedes- dry heaves, chills, drowning in
shame- if you knew, you would get me a dose. You would.

The doctor droned on. My mama leaned in. The doctor
dug out journals and charts. While they were busy
I stole a prescription pad. Right off the desk. Right
down my pants. My mama thanked the doctor.

She is through crying, she says, she is ready
to fight. My mama is fired up. I promised to try
to be what she wants me to be. And I meant it.

I took the blank scripts to Sonny. I didn't know how
to turn that pad into pills. Sonny gave me this shit free
for helping him out. See we are a community, and I am
part of something, and y'all need to leave me alone

'cause I'm in the ocean now, and it's all warm, this is love,
I could do anything, it's all good, I am where I belong and
the waves are crashing over my head and I've never been
this far before, floating away, I feel kind of separate

from my body now and the waves are crashing over
my head and I see my mama way down on the shore,
she is crying again and slapping my face but I'm way out,
flowing away and now I'm just waving good bye, good bye.

—*Elizabeth S. Wolf*

SHE FELL ASLEEP

in geometry. The only shape and size
she was concerned with was that which filled
her bra cup. She knew as soon as each test ended
that she would soon forget it. One doesn't retain

the material that's taught in high-school. What is
retained isn't stuffed in notes or learned in class.
That is self-confidence, a sense of belonging and
accomplishment. She knew even straight A

students struggled with this. Those were the ones
that so many demands were put upon, the ones
that starved themselves, cut themselves and bled,
some to their death. What was behind the scene

was scarier yet. These were the molested ones, beaten
with sticks and belts, passed out mothers on the couch,
absentee fathers, late night at work, empty refrigerators.
Fill your head with points and lines

until you lose your mind. Cover the bruises with
make-up. Wear layers so as not to show your protruding
bones. Drink black coffee for the hang-over. Just don't
fall asleep in geometry.

—Sandra Wylie

PULL OF THE POET

You're not attracted to him
Of course you're not
You're married
Paradoxically he's separated and says
you're the most attractive woman he's ever met

Whispers compliments in your ears in public places
Writes poems about you in private
Reads them plenty loud in public
Takes notes on nearly everything you say
Snaps pictures and insists he doesn't see
that one of your eyes is smaller than the other

Comes back periodically to gauge his progress
A patient person whose confidence
could possibly compensate
for lack of chemistry

But you're not attracted to him
Of course you're not
You're married
It's those pesky poems
that pulled him into last night's dream

Like a cluster fly on exposed body parts
crawling south to warmer locales
And you didn't swat him away
Because your unconscious didn't know
you're not attracted to him
Of course you're not
You're married

—Ellaraine Lockie

TO WALT WHITMAN

Dear Walt Whitman, I won't forget
your wild, your hawk,
"Beneath my feet the blades of grass"
Not circling high with the hawk
but exhaling, the earth pulling
stubby too-soon-cut red grasses
bending easily beneath the step
giving up their sweet savory breath
to the damp of your boot sole dirt
How did the daisy wrap itself around that rock
to greet me
as the afternoon wind
Surges the sumacs towards the ground?

My footsteps, fragile, touch upon the earth
leaving broken wisps
as cumulus clouds mound in the distance
threatening something yet unknown
to wash the face of settlings
transform the unexpected to be now
this moment, a flicker
the flap of a bird's wing
shiver of light
breaking into full flight
beyond the folding velvet hills
and the dark canyons of purple roars
into the dry brown fingers folded against the flat reaches
To feel the warm caress of
the air that rises from those reaches
and to live in the centuries folded one upon the other
and soar into that beyond
with the smell of dirt still clinging.

—Sandra Thaxter

BEACH PLUMS

In last melancholy moments of summer,
tenuously balanced on a border:
departure of season's long languid hours,
arrival of preparations and uncertainty
where air has cooled but sun still warms.
Now picking beach plums—
red-purple fruit, perfectly round,
color of late evening's last light,
smaller than a cherry but
bigger than a blueberry,
on a tree, diminutive and gnarled,
with gray, lichen-laced branches
on back edge of dune.
It has weathered winter winds,
blowing sand and salt spray
to produce an abundance,
too sour to eat, so jelly is made.
Bounty boiled down to
a deep garnet-hued liquid
that shimmers like a jewel
in its clear crystal jar.
The taste, wild and plummy,
decidedly not domesticated
with a hint of sea air.
Autumn brings renewed tasks,
but after indolence of long light,
I am not at all prepared
and can only focus
on the harvest of beach plums
to bring the memory of summer's sun,
something shiny and sweet,
into the darkening days.

—*Lainie Senechal*

STRAGGLERS

The upside down face of Captain Kangaroo
I woke to years ago on a couch behind
unfamiliar children watching TV, my terror
that all I drank at a wedding rehearsal
the night before had scrambled
my ocular equipment. I was the straggler
then, and that was one kind of astonishment,
but these days it's more likely to be
a sparrow bedraggled by three days of rain,
a wild underhang of feathers
below its tricolor brown, black and white,
until I notice the bird's way too hefty,
the beak's pink and wrong, and that's
not a sparrow's grab-and-go at the feeder.
It is hanging around as if lost, a blow-in
on a northeast storm who has followed
the locals to a seed source, its white eyestripe
and lunula at first perhaps a Peabody bird's,
then another kind of astonishment:
it may be a rarity from one of those islands
where puffins are a food staple
instead of a postcard. Good enough,
but just once more I wish another
memorable face were studying my sleep
through the window screen at Long Pond,
a foot away and taking me in so benignly
that ever since I've believed
St Francis had a dog called Brother Beagle.

—Brendan Galvin

HOW FAST IS A ROCK POOL?

How Fast is a rock pool?
      Tiny fish making a dash – a split second.
      Crab scuttling to a new rock – a second
      Hermit crab going for an RV trip of 2 inches – 3 seconds
      Moon Snail out for a slide – 1 minute
      Moon Snail preparing supper – 5 hours
      The tide covering the pool – 6 hours
      Many more things of many speeds: starfish, anemones, urchins and weeds.

A whole world of life moving at many speeds.

On the first hand – It's more than:

      I love to search in rock pools,
      Those peaceful little things
      Just tiny scurrying creatures
      With fins instead of wings.

      Scurrying isn't really the way to go,
      Certain snails are very slow
      And they are not the slowest things
      Do Sea Anemones have wings?

      It's soothing, the roar of waves you miss
      In the glory of this oasis
      What a quiet restful place
      Held serene in God's good grace.

      The Moon snail is so beautiful,
      Supreme shell on magnificent pad
      To see it gliding makes you glad
      Ahh peace…

On the other hand:

      The rock pool is a gladiatorial ring
      With everything eating everything.
      The drillers line up for their next meal
      and, in order to get there desired filling
      they set the bit for 5 hours drilling.
      The bit's not diamond – it's a rasping tongue
      Drilling a hole in every one.
      And when the perfect hole is there
      Ingestion feeds the juices fair.

      Moon snails are the biggest borers

With dog winkles coming close behind.
Periwinkles are on the lettuce farm
Which mostly keeps them out of harm.

Starfish they seem pretty nice,
But, suctioned to a mussel, they don't think twice
As the muscles of their orange feet
Open the mussel and serve the treat.

So in this world that seemed so simple
There are many worlds of many times.
A long slow look and you'll see more
Of the lives upon the shore. .

—Peter Bryant

THE LUCK QUARRY DUMP

It was a half-mile from my house.
Saturdays, after chores, after homework,
I'd bicycle there to walk among old stoves

and wide appliances where cold came
boxed behind doors, taken off now, set aside,
so rain pooled stagnant where food was kept.

There was smaller wreckage—a bicycle
mangled, rims akimbo; leather luggage
flung open, silk pockets given over

to metallic flash of green lizards.
TV sets, broken lamps, yellow shades
wattage burned through; mattresses—

quilting ripped, the brown batting, coils
rising like wild rusty underlings set free.
Sometimes I'd lean the great black halo

of a Good Year tractor tire against a tree
and curl myself inside. I felt at home
here among the replaceable.

—Grey Held

DARK SIDE OF THE POND

Prepare for a launch
from the surface,
rippling and reflecting.

The countdown, inaudible, comes
from the diaphragm: *three...two...one:*
one last deep breath to last
the length of this journey

beginning now with toes
pointing, disappearing from the view
of a horizontal lap-swimmer,
appearing soon to the
unblinking eyes of brown trout

ten feet down, passed by on
this simple trip progressing into cool
blue, blue-green, dark grey,
darkness.

The scene through goggles
15 feet below and still
descending is a journey through
deep space: reference points gone,
velocity uncertain, countless luminous
particles suspended passing
as a film of distant stars
bending time.

Keep the trajectory with kicks
and palm-thrusts—
this soaring, climbing down
now a feeling
of leaving the earth,
inverted ascent a working
against buoyancy, not gravity.

At 18 feet below, the destination—
the stark, silent bottom of Walden Pond—
looms into dim-lit view; at

20 feet, the ice-water line of the thermocline
offers its full-body embrace. The mission:
find one fine rock to bring up from this
lunar-like landscape, pulling it

from the slow-motion swirling
silt, where it's been half-buried, glacier-
dropped, waiting in time since before
time was given a name.

(Hours or years later this rock will become
a sculpture, a precious stone, a talisman.)

Now stand to survey this peaceful land.

Now push off from 22 feet down to
make the return trip, swimming
toward widening light above with
one free, non-stone-cradling hand.

Now splash-up into the world
of trains, trees, voices and air.

Breath held must be released,
but the rock retrieved can be held always,
itself now held with a length of twine
(equal to the depth where it was found)

wrapped around it securely—reminder
of another, other-worldly realm:
that aquatic, imperturbable,
almost-dark-side-of-the-moon.

—*Kirk Etherton*

KIMONO CITY

The fabric of this kimono
is silver-gray
thick-woven,
weighty, enduring,
crisscrossed with threads that outline
squares and rectangles
some small, some wide,
some tall, some overlapping.

The fabric of this city
is ancient, patched with care,
new mingled with the old.

From a height,
observe the patterns of charcoal and pewter
edging squares of taupe and white–
buildings constructed of cubes,
side by side and in stacked tiers,
matte wood and stone,
glinting roof tiles.

Turn the eyes, and
scenes flicker—
light reflecting from every flat surface,
shadows forming in recesses.

Turn the head, and
streets appear and disappear behind
slatted fences, shrines, signboards,
elevated roadways.

Walk down a street to discover
hidden alleys, paths intersecting, gutters, canals
making a checkered pattern,
planned, with intentional asymmetries,
natural, as in hand-woven cloth.

This creation, which at a distance
seemed a neat, folded package,
spreads its sleeves
as you draw closer,
opening outwards from
collar to hem, revealing

a lining of soft jade and

luminous emerald
floating on metallic liquid,
the weave infused with tufts of narrow, bright threads:
rice fields, wildflowers and grasses
that sprout and bloom,
planted at different times—

interwoven among the buildings, blocks, and streets,
the shimmering ever-changing patterns of green
startle the eye in their intensity,
seeming to emerge more brilliantly
every time the kimono opens.

I want to clothe myself in this robe,
strong on the outside, smooth-textured inside—
to fit myself gently and surely into its shape,
to wrap my waist securely
in an obi sash of history,

to rest and walk every day
in this intricate, artful design—
to wear it as my city.

—Lucy Holstedt

BOTTOM OF THE BOTTLE

He was looking through the bottom of the bottle
at the drunks on the Boston Common
through the bottom at the druggies with needles
through the bottom at the hoity-toity with briefcases
through the bottom at himself

He had been at the top, been on top of her before
she left him for the governor whose wife was already
dead and where he wanted to be but he found the
bottle easier merlot and chardonnay his pals
the world looked so different through the bottom of the bottle

red to see the dead the ones who never return
white for the world of friends who slept on the Boston Common benches
and in the Public Gardens the flowers died
slower than the friends he knew through the bottom of the bottle
while back at the Boston Common he watched them slowly fade away

In the winter his ear lobes could have fallen off but for the Pine Street Inn rescue
in summer the police scooted him out of the Common so he slept in the alleys
where he was rolled for the buck or two or kids would find his bottle
pour it over him or if lucky he would roll on top of some woman
then look at her again through the bottom of the bottle

Blessed are the drunkards who survive their days in hell
and think that heaven is a bottle that brings them close to God
but then it is done and over and they recover or they lose
there may be time to recall the past and the bottom of the bottle
the bottom of the bottle where his life began and ended.

—Zvi A. Sesling

WAYNE SPEAKS

it is a protocol
the thing with mass shooters
the rule the precedence
is that the shooter hisself gets shot
killed
and that's that
after one news cycle
nada
now this stupid kid in Florida
an aberration
after the shooting
goes to Subway gets a sandwich
does not go down fighting
but rather gets caught
hires a fancy pants lawyer
and he'll be in the news forever
with trial and sentencing
and conviction plus appeal
henceforth forevermore
I am saying
we need some justice here
do you know
some idiot with a weapon?
it better not be a firearm
a knife   maybe an icepick?
what was it killed Trotsky?
that would be good
if it's a firearm
we might get blamed for it

—*Michael Casey*

WHERE YOU WERE

Friday, 10:30 a.m. PST, when gunshots
stilled the earth's spin: At school
carefully printing alphabet letters
between the paper's dotted blue lines,
sounding out words about Puff and Spot.
After lunch the teachers, looking grave,
agreed "assassination" was a word
above your comprehension level.

Friday, 2:30 p.m. PST, Air Force One en route
to Washington: On Bus Number 5, KFXM blaring,
Lesley Gore wailing that you'd cry, too,
if it happened to you. At your stop you charged off,
heedless of Don the Bus Driver's sad head-shake,
barreling with your playmates into their house.
Their mother and sister, glued to the TV,
shushed the three of you: "The President's been shot."

Saturday, 8:00 a.m. PST: In your room, aggrieved
that Saturday morning cartoons weren't on,
even the ones you didn't normally watch.
You ran out to check the TV again just in case,
but every channel featured men talking, talking,
talking in somber tones. Your parents were silent,
grim-faced. You did not understand, even after
your brother and sister said, "no school on Monday."

Monday, 8:30 a.m. PST: On the living room couch,
your only previous experience of death a phone call
that made your mother cry. On TV a mass of people
marched solemnly behind a flag-draped coffin
led by a black-veiled woman. Earlier you glimpsed her
holding the hands of two children. Your mother tried
to explain, but you were still uncertain, confused.
You didn't know it, but so was the rest of the country.

—Patricia L. Hamilton

RAGE ON THE THIRD FLOOR

A city outside Boston, 2015

He bludgeoned her one year ago, then fled
though killed by cops responding to the scene—
the 911 call by the oldest son.
The bat the father used, exhibit A,
put mother in a coma for two months,
the kids all sent away to foster homes.
Most hits were to her head. He'd thought her dead
so left the house, she sprawled, alone until
the kids came home to find her on the floor,
blood pooled and wet. They saw. They saved her life—
she's blind, she limps, she's tired and she forgets.
Her PCA is with her every day—
just four hours: to wash, make meals, give meds.
She falls a lot, but now she feels she's safe.

—*Paulette Demers Turco*

THE BIG KID

He was the biggest kid in a class
of forty kids—row after row.
Always ready to harass
his fellow classmates just for show.

They, in turn, would tease him cruelly;
hide his books and lessons, trip
his big feet in the hallway, rudely
taunting him. He'd give back *lip*.

The nuns would warn him to behave,
blame mostly him for causing an uproar,
then put him—which was more depraved?—
in a locker, shut the door.

Then they'd make us bow and pray.
Later, his family moved away.

—Priscilla Turner Spada

A TEACHER

I want to be A Teacher.
I want to fill their minds with curiosity, not
Fill their wounds with my thumb to slow their dying.
I want to give their classroom endless books, not
Give their corpses to wailing parents and green-faced medics.
I want to clean their souls of prejudice and hate, not
Clean their blood from desks and tile floors.
I want to hear their speeches on slavery, ancestors, and novels, not
Hear their screaming as shot after shot Slays the prom queen.
Slays the theatre kid.
Slays your kid.
Slays me.

I want to love and save our children, not
From searing bullets, but
From a future without potential.
You must love and save our children first.
From your Senators, and
From lobbyists without ethics.

I want to be A Teacher.
For all of us, let me TEACH.

—Jim Kelly

OLD LANG SIGN
for David Lang

The little man pedaled as fast as he could
so the big wheels turned,
though it really didn't make any difference,
since they did not touch the ground.
The gently moving wings above
would take him wherever he wanted
on his endless journey,
the Cat explained to Alice.

They continued on their way
in the Cat's cart, which was
driven by a reciprocating engine
with seven cylinders fashioned
from vegetable juice containers.
It wobbled a little unevenly,
not having a balanced set.
"I could have had a V8,"
the Cat explained regretfully.

They moved past Charades hospital
with a kinetic sign that indicated
the illness special of the day:
six pigs with flapping wings.
"Swine flew/flu," explained the Cat.

But then the Cat started to fade away,
leaving only his smile as a memory.
"Please come back," cried Alice,
"David, please come back."

—Keith Tornheim

GOOD WILL

We give ourselves away. We give the shirts
styled for a decade, donned a day, still wearing
tags—*Dockers, Dior*—of selves
outgrown or only glanced at, to hang
for bargainers' scrutiny on tight racks. Will
choosers be beggars for looks
in the mirror, thumbs up
in hand-me-downs? We browse for pocket
rather than collar or cuff, digging
our treasures from others' discards,
itch as they may. Finders
keepers, with wide eyes: *Can you believe…*
as simultaneously across town
with equal remorse: *How could I have
let go of that Polo?* Of the senses
(with cents) you count, your taste
for plums comforts others. Your touch
withdraws in the XLs. Your eyes
are burning holes through me. More dire
acceptance steps softly. *If the shoe fits—*
Cinderella, Seuss, disguised for the meanwhile.

—*Michael Todd Steffen*

Kathleen Aguero's latest book of poetry is *After That*. She teaches in the low-residency M.F.A. in creative writing program at Pine Manor College and in Changing Lives through Literature, an alternative sentencing program. She also conducts creative writing for caregivers workshops privately and through adult and community education centers.

Nina Rubinstein Alonso's poetry appeared in *The New Yorker, Ploughshares, Bagel Bards, Ibbetson Street, Cambridge Artists' Cooperative, Wilderness House Review, Muddy River Poetry Review, MomEgg, University of Massachusetts Review,* and *Constant Remembrance*. Her stories were in *Southern Women's Review, Tears and Laughter, Broadkill Review, Black Poppy Review,* etc. David Godine Press published her book *This Body*, and her chapbook *Riot Wake* will be published by Cervena Barva Press.

Jennifer Barber's poetry collections are *Works on Paper* (The Word Works, 2016), *Given Away* (Kore Press, 2012), and *Rigging the* Wind (Kore Press, 2003). Her poems have appeared in the *New Yorker,* the *Missouri Review, Poetry, Poetry Daily,* the *Harvard Divinity Bulletin,* and elsewhere. She received the 2017 Isabella Gardner Fellowship from the MacDowell Colony. She edits the literary journal *Salamander* at Suffolk University, where she also teaches.

Molly Mattfield Bennett has published in several magazines including *Knock, Antioch* (Seattle), *Ibbetson Street, Constellations, Off the Coast, and Solstice*. In 2010 *Name the Glory* was published by Wilderness House Press, and in June 2012 she read at the Jeff Male Memorial Reading at the William Joiner Institutes' Writers Conference, University of Massachusetts. Her book *Point-No-Point* was published in 2016 by FutureCycle Press.

Denise Bergman is the author of *A Woman in Pieces Crossed a Sea, The Telling,* and *Seeing Annie Sullivan*. She conceived and edited the anthology *City River of Voices*. A stanza of her poem about a neighborhood near a slaughterhouse is installed in a public park in Cambridge, Massachusetts. Poems are forthcoming in *Beloit Poetry Journal, Paterson Review,* and the Syracuse Cultural Workers calendar, and appeared recently in *Poetry, Salamander, Solstice,* and other journals.

Jessie Brown (www.JessieBrown.net is the author of two short collections, *What We Don't Know We Know* (Finishing Line Press) and *Lucky* (Anabiosis Press). Her poems and translations have appeared in local and national journals such as *The Comstock Review, New Madrid, Minerva Rising,* and the *American Poetry Review*. She leads independent writing workshops as well as poetry programs for schools and communities in the greater Boston area. She also develops interdisciplinary projects incorporating poetry and the visual arts. A founding member of the Alewife Poets, she gives frequent performances both in collaboration and alone.

Peter Bryant writes both freestyle and form. Inspired by poetry events at the Blue Wave Studio in Amesbury he started a series of ekphrastic poems. These graduated from paintings into interpretations of photographs, and then deeper into the stories behind the photographs—sometimes adventures—sometimes natural facts—as those gleaned about rock pools. Peter has spent many happy hours splashing around in rock pools, catching, but not really looking. A deeper dive into rock pools made Peter aware of the worlds involved—hence this poem.

Mary Buchinger, author of *Navigating the Reach*, (forthcoming), einfühlung/*in feeling* (2018), *Aerialist* (2015), and *Roomful of Sparrows* (2008), is President of the New England Poetry Club and Professor of English and Communication Studies at MCPHS University in Boston; her work has appeared in *AGNI, Gargoyle, Nimrod, Salamander,* and elsewhere.

John Canaday is the author of *Critical Assembly*, a collection of poems in the voices of the men and women—scientists, spouses, laborers, locals, and military personnel—involved in the Manhattan Project. His previous book of poems, *The Invisible World*, set in the Middle East and New England, won the Walt Whitman Award from the Academy of American Poets. He is also the author of a nonfiction study, *The Nuclear Muse: Literature, Physics, and the First Atomic Bombs*.

Jo Carney Jo Carney's multi-media life led from theatre to jazz singer to writing three novels of historical fiction and non-fiction adventure through Alaska. Her poetry has been featured in several anthologies and in *Shenandoah* and *Ibbetson Street*.

Michael Casey is the author of *There It Is: New & Selected Poems* from Paul Marion's Loom Press of Lowell, Massachusetts.

Ruth Chad is a psychologist who lives and works in the Boston area. Her poems have appeared in the *Aurorean, Bagels with the Bards, Connection, The Psychoanalytic Couple and Family Institute of New England, Constellations, Ibbetson Street* and several others. Her chapbook, *The Sound of Angels* is pending publication by Cervena Barva Press in 2017.

Avi Chad-Friedman is a data scientist and software engineer from Newton, Massachusetts living in Los Angeles. He started writing during his senior year at Columbia. *Ibbetson Street* is the first publication his writing has appeared in. Other than that, he has a collection of poems and short stories gathering dust on his Google drive. His hobbies include exploring events in Los Angeles and complaining about Los Angeles.

Laura Cherry is the author of the collection *Haunts* (Cooper Dillon Books) and the chapbooks *Two White Beds* (Minerva Rising) and *What We Planted* (Providence Athenaeum). She co-edited the anthology *Poem, Revised* (Marion Street Press). Her work has been published in journals including *Antiphon, Clementine Poetry Journal, Los Angeles Review, Cider Press Review, Tuesday; An Art Project,* and *H_NGM_N.*

Llyn Clague is a poet based in Hastings-on-Hudson, NY. His poems have been published widely, including in *Ibbetson Street, Atlanta Review, Wisconsin Review, California Quarterly, Main Street Rag, New York Quarterly,* and other magazines. His seventh book, *Hard-Edged and Childlike*, was published by Main Street Rag in September, 2014. Visit www.llynclague.com.

Louisa Clerici's stories and poetry have been published in literary anthologies and magazines including *Best New England Crime Stories, Carolina Woman, Pink Panther Magazine and Muddy River Poetry Review*. Her work was chosen for the Massachusetts Poetry Festival's Poetry & the Body, Raining Poetry Program. Her articles on the South Shore art scene appear in local newspapers. Louisa works as a therapist and sleep educator at Clear Mind Systems in Plymouth, Massachusetts: www.clearmindsystems.net.

Dennis Daly has published six books of poetry and poetic translations. He has recently published reviews in *Ibbetson Street, The Notre Dame Review,* and the *Somerville Times*. Daly's translation of Sophocles' *Ajax* was recently performed at Skidmore College. Visit Daly's blog, Weights and Measures, at dennisfdaly.blogspot.com.

Beatriz Alba Del Rio is a bilingual poet and lawyer and a life member of the New England Poetry Club. Beatriz has won the international poetry contests of Octavio Paz and Pablo Neruda and others, i.e. Cambridge Poetry Prizes. Her translations were awarded the Diana Der Hovanessian Prize by the New England Poetry Club. Her poetry has appeared in several anthologies and literary magazines. Beatriz's mission as a lawyer is to strongly advocate for underprivileged kids' and parents' rights and inspire them to re-create better lives. Her poetry speaks of longings, of clash of cultures, of the oneness of us all. Her poetry is a song to love and life's absurdities and wonders. (badelrio@comcast.net)

Susan Demarest teaches English at Bunker Hill Community College in Boston. Her feature articles on antiques have appeared in *Antiques and Collectibles* and her poems have appeared in *Hawaii Review, Tar River Poetry, Gargoyle*, and *Merrimac Mic Anthology*. Her humanities blog is at trouverses.net.

Wendy Drexler's third poetry collection, *Before There Was Before,* was published by Iris Press in March 2017. A three-time Pushcart-Prize nominee, her poems have appeared in *Barrow Street, J Journal, Nimrod, Prairie Schooner, Salamander, The Maine Review, The Mid-American Review, The Hudson Review, The Worcester Review*, and the *Valparaiso Poetry Review,* among others. She lives in Belmont, Massachusetts, with her husband and two formerly feral cats.

Kirk Etherton works as a freelance ad writer, and has done award-winning work for a wide variety of clients. He also coordinates, promotes, and hosts various events—including the Boston National Poetry Month Festival (he is a board member). As a songwriter, Kirk's "best" tune may be the one about an ancient fish. His creating art from submerged stones (see poem in this issue) led him to be a featured artist on WGBH's "All Things Considered" in 2017.

Linda M. Fischer has poems published or forthcoming in *the Aurorean, Innisfree Poetry Journal, Iodine Poetry Journal, Muddy River Poetry Review, Poetry East, Potomac Review, Roanoke Review, Schuylkill Valley Journal, Valparaiso Poetry Review, Verse-Virtual, Wilderness House Literary Review, The Worcester Review*, and elsewhere. For more poetry and information on her chapbooks *Raccoon Afternoons* and *Glory:* lindamfischer.com.

Brendan Galvin is the author of eighteen collections of poems. *Habitat: New and Selected Poems 1965-2005* (LSU Press) was a finalist for the National Book Award. *The Air's Accomplices*, a collection of new poems, is available from LSU Press now, and *Egg Island Almanac* will appear from Southern Illinois University Press in fall, 2017. He lives in Truro, Massachusetts.

Harris Gardner's credits: *The Harvard Review; A Poet's Siddur; Constellations; Midstream; Cool Plums; Rosebud; Fulcrum; Chest; Ibbetson Street;; Vallum* (Canada); and over fifty others. Three collections. Poetry Editor, *Ibbetson Street*: 2010 to present; co-founder: Tapestry of Voices and Boston National Poetry Month Festival with Lainie Senechal. Member: four Poet Laureate selection committees: Boston, Somerville. Recipient of Ibbetson Street Life Time Achievement Award - 2015. Citation from Massachusetts House of Representatives - 2015.

Literary Performer, **Regie O'Hare Gibson**, has lectured and performed in the U.S. and abroad and received the Absolute Poetry Award in Monfalcone, Italy. He has been featured on WBUR's On Point, Radio Boston & published in *Poetry* Magazine, Harvard's *Divinity* Magazine, and *The Iowa Review*. He has received the Walker Scholarship from the Provincetown FAWC and a 2018 Brother Thomas Fellowship for Artistic Excellence from The Boston Foundation.

This is **Eric Greinke**'s third *Ibbetson Street* appearance. Other new work is in *Cape Rock Poetry, Freshwater Literary Journal, Gargoyle, Lake Effect, Lilipoh, Paterson Literary Review, Plainsongs* and *Trajectory*. New in 2018: *Shorelines* (Adastra Press), *Masterplan - Collaborative Poems*, with Alison Stone (Presa Press). Contributing Writer, *Schuylkill Valley Journal*. www.ericgreinke.com.

Patricia L. Hamilton is a professor of English in Jackson, Tennessee. She has work forthcoming in *Poem, Broad River Review, Homestead Review, Third Wednesday,* and *Sarasvati* and new work in *Split Rock Review, Red River Review, Soul-Lit,* and *Valley Voices*. She won the Rash Award in Poetry in 2015 and 2017 and has received 3 Pushcart nominations. *The Distance to Nightfall*, her first collection, was published by Main Street Rag in 2014.

Grey Held is a recipient of a National Endowment for the Arts Fellowship in Creative Writing. Two of his books of poems have been published, *Two-Star General* (by Brick Road Poetry Press in 2012) and *Spilled Milk* (by Word Press in 2013), and a third, *WORKaDAY*, is forthcoming in 2019 from FutureCycle Press. He works closely with the Mayor's Office of Cultural Affairs in Newton, Massachusetts to direct projects that connect contemporary poets (and their poetry) with a wider audience.

Carol Hobbs is a poet from Newfoundland who lives, writes, and teaches in Massachusetts. Her work has appeared in journals, magazines, and anthologies in Canada, Ireland, and the United States. Most recently she has published with the *3 Nations Anthology*, a collection of work from Native American, New England, and Atlantic Canadian poets, and she presented her work in company with these poets at the Massachusetts Poetry Festival in May 2018. Her book manuscript, *New Found Lande*, received a PEN New England Discovery Prize.

Richard Hoffman is the author of the memoirs *Half the House* and *Love & Fury*. In addition to the volume, *Interference and Other Stories*, he has published four collections of poetry, *Without Paradise; Gold Star Road; Emblem*; and *Noon until Night*. He is Senior Writer in Residence at Emerson College and an Adjunct Associate Professor in the Graduate Writing Program at Columbia University.

Lucy Holstedt is a professor at Berklee College of Music and founding director of Women Musicians Network. As board member of the Boston National Poetry Month Festival, she produces the website and an annual evening of Poetry, Music and Dance. Lucy composes and performs poem settings, choral works, and solo music. Her current sabbatical project is a collection of original arrangements and translations of Japanese children's songs.

Barbara Helfgott Hyett has five collections of poetry. *Rift* (2008: University of Arkansas Press) was awarded the Brother Thomas Fellowship for Excellence in the Arts by the Boston Foundation. Winner of many other prizes and awards, Barbara has taught English and poetry at Boston University, Harvard University, MIT and Holy Cross, and is the director of PoemWorks: the Workshop for Publishing Poets.

Now retired, **Robert K. Johnson**, was a Professor of English at Suffolk University in Boston for many years. For eight years, he was also the Poetry Editor of *Ibbetson Street* magazine. His poems have appeared in a wide variety of magazines and newspapers both here and abroad. The most recent collections of his poetry are *From Mist to Shadow* and *Choir Of Day*.

Judy Katz-Levine's new collection of poems, *The Everything Saint,* will be published by WordTech in the fall of 2018. Her previous collections include *Ocarina* and *When The Arms Of Our Dreams Embrace. When Performers Swim, The Dice Are Cast,* is her most recent chapbook. Poems have appeared recently in *Salamander, Event Horizon, Blue Unicorn, Unlikely Stories Mark, Writing In A Woman's Voice, Miriam's Well,* and other journals. Her translations of Rimbaud and Henri Michaux appear in *Salamander* and *Blue Unicorn.*

Jim Kelly is an undergraduate student at Endicott College pursuing a BA in History and a minor in Philosophy. He hopes to teach in the high school classroom.

Lawrence Kessenich won the 2010 Strokestown International Poetry Prize. His poetry has been published in *Sewanee Review, Atlanta Review, Poetry Ireland Review,* and many other magazines. Three of his poems were read on NPR's *The Writer's* Almanac and three nominated for the Pushcart Prize. He has published two chapbooks, *Strange News* and *Pearl*, two full-length books, *Before Whose Glory* and *Age of Wonders*, and a novel, *Cinnamon Girl*. All of his books are available at lawrence-writer.com.

Ted Kooser's most recent collection is *Kindest Regards: New and Selected Poems*, from Copper Canyon Press. His fourth children's picture book, *Mr. Posey's New Glasses* is due out from Candlewick Press in the fall of 2018. He lives in rural Nebraska and teaches writing at the University of Nebraska in Lincoln.

Rona Laban has been an editor for a published novelist, as well as a copywriter. Her poem, "My Father's Plant Stand," was nominated for a 2017 Pushcart Prize. Two of her poems were in the Fall 2017 edition of the *Muddy River Poetry Review*. She has been in three anthologies, including the *Bagel Bards Anthology*. Her haikus have appeared in *Extracts*. She has been a feature at the Mike Amado Art of Words in Plymouth, Massachusetts.

Ellaraine Lockie's *Tripping with the Top Down* is her thirteenth chapbook. Earlier collections have won Poetry Forum's Chapbook Contest Prize, San Gabriel Valley Poetry Festival Chapbook Competition, Encircle Publications Chapbook Contest, Best Individual Poetry Collection Award from *Purple Patch* magazine in England, and the *Aurorean's* Chapbook Choice Award. Ellaraine has received multiple nominations for the Pushcart Prize, teaches writing workshops and serves as Poetry Editor for the lifestyles magazine, *Lilipoh*.

Ann McCrea lives in Newburyport, where she studies with Rhina Espaillat and participates in a workshop with Alfred Nicol. She reads regularly at the Pow Wow River Poets' open mic. Recently she gave a presentation of her haiku and the eighteenth century Japanese paintings that inspired them at the Joppa Audubon Center. Her poetry has appeared in *Merrimac Mic Anthology II*, *Merrimac Mic Anthology IV*, and *The Aurorean*. In her artist's booklet, *Walking Haiku*, she combines her haiku with her collages.

Susan Lloyd McGarry has published poetry in several small magazines and gives readings and workshops. Her poems have been anthologized in *The Poetry of Peace* and *Beyond Raised Voices*. Named Bard of the Boston Irish Festival for her poem, "Memory of Coumeenole," she read there to more than 1000 people. She writes and edits material for center devoted to health and human rights; she also works as a freelance editor. Former managing editor of the *Harvard Divinity Bulletin*, she edited their poetry issue, *The Radiant Imagination*.

Triona McMorrow lives in Dunlaoghaire, County Dublin. She was shortlisted for the International Francis Ledwidge Poetry competition in 2009 and 2011. She was shortlisted for The Galway University Hospitals Arts Trust poetry competition in 2013. She has had poems published in *Ibbetson Street* journal in Boston, Massachusetts. In 2014, The Bealtaine group, of which she is a member, published an anthology of poetry titled *Bealtaine*.

Ed Meek is the author of *Spy Pond*, poems, and *Luck*, short stories. He has had poems in *The Sun, Plume, The Paris Review*, etc. He writes book reviews for *The Arts Fuse* and *Digboston*. He teaches creative writing at the Cambridge Center for Adult Education and helps adults prepare for the high School Equivalency Exam at X-Cel Education.

Gary Metras's new book of poetry is *White Storm* (Presa Press 2018), with another book, *Captive in the Here*, due soon from Cervena Barva Press. The author of sixteen previous collections of poetry, his poems have appeared in *America, The Common, Poetry, Poetry East*, and *Poetry Salzburg Review*. He lives in Easthampton, Massachusetts, where he has recently been appointed the city's first Poet Laureate.

Tomas O'Leary— s poetry career began at age four when he sneezed and accidentally rhymed it with canoe. He has taught literature and writing at college, high school and elementary levels. For over 20 years he has worked with Alzheimer's groups, conversing, singing, playing accordion. His published volumes are *Fool at the Funeral, The Devil Take a Crooked House, A Prayer for Everyone*, and most recently a "new & selected" called *In the Wellspring of the Ear*.

Denise Provost has written poetry for many years. She has published in online and print journals, including Bagel Bards anthologies, *Ibbetson Street*, *Muddy River Poetry Review*, *qarrtsiluni*, *Quadrille*, *Poetry Porch's Sonnet Scroll*, *Sanctuary*, and *Light Quarterly*. Provost lives in Somerville, Massachusetts.

Gayle Roby Gayle Roby received an MFA in Poetry from Warren Wilson College. Her work has appeared in several journals, including *The Iowa Review*, *The Ohio Review*, *Prairie Schooner*, and *Ibbetson Street*. She is a member of the Alewife Poets, and lives in Arlington, Massachusetts with her husband, son and cats.

Hilary Sallick is the author of a chapbook, *Winter Roses* (Finishing Line Press, 2017), and a full-length collection, *Asking the Form*, to be published by Cervena Barva Press. Her poems have appeared recently or are forthcoming in *Whiskey Island*, *The Inflectionist Review*, *Two Cities Review*, *Third Wednesday*, and other publications. She teaches reading and writing to adult learners in Somerville, MA, and she is vice-president of the New England Poetry Club.

Bridget Seley-Galway, artist/poet, received a Chancellor full merit scholarship at the University of Massachusetts-Amherst and the Binney Smith Artistic Achievement award. She earned BFAs in painting and Art Education. Her poems have been published in Provincetown Magazine Poetry Corner, Bagels with the Bards anthologies, *Popt Art* magazine, *Ibbetson Street*, *Wilderness House Literary Review*, *Soul-Lit*, *Poetry Porch*, and *Somerville Times*. Her art has exhibited throughout New England and been reviewed and printed in *Artist Magazine*, *Cape Cod Review*, *Cape Arts Magazine*, *Popt Art*, and *Emerson's Redivider*. Her paintings have been selected for the covers of Bagel with Bards Anthology, several issues of *Ibbetson Street*, Doug Holder's *Eating Grief at 3 AM* and Molly Lynn Watt's *On the Wings of Song, A journey into the Civil Rights Era*.

Lainie Senechal, poet, painter and environmentalist, has read and featured at many venues throughout New England. She is the former poet laureate of Amesbury, Massachusetts. Her poetry has appeared in journals and anthologies including *The Aurorean*, *Dasoku*, *Ibbetson Street*, *Spare Change*, *Wilderness House Literary Review*, *The Larcom Review*, *The South Boston Literary Gazette*, *City of Poets*. She co-authored two volumes of poetry. Her most recent chapbook is *Vocabulary of Awakening*.

Zvi A. Sesling is the Poet Laureate of Brookline, MA. He edits *Muddy River Poetry Review*, publishes *Muddy River Books* and reviews for *Boston Small Press and Poetry Scene*. He is author of The *Lynching of Leo Frank*, *Fire Tongue* and *King of the Jungle* and two chapbooks *Love Poems From Hell* and *Across Stones of Bad Dreams*. His next book, *War Zones*, is due out from Nixes Mate Books.

Lee Sharkey is the author of *Walking Backwards* (Tupelo, 2016), *Calendars of Fire* (Tupelo, 2013), *A Darker, Sweeter String* (Off the Grid, 2008), and eight earlier full-length poetry collections and chapbooks. Her poetry has appeared in *Consequence*, *Crazyhorse*, *FIELD*, *Kenyon Review*, *Massachusetts Review*, *Seattle Review*, and other journals. Her recognitions include the Ballymaloe International Poetry Prize and the Abraham Sutzkever Centennial Translation Prize.

Priscilla Turner Spada lives in Newburyport, Massachusetts. She has a chapbook, *Light in Unopened Windows, Finishing Line Press, 2016*. Other publications include: *Ibbetson Street* #'s 40, 41,42; *Merrimac Mic Anthologies II and IV*; *Wingbeats II*, Dos Gatos Press; *What is Home?*, Portsmouth Poet Laureate Program. She is a regular reader at the Powow River Poets; Merrimac Mic; Amesbury library; Portsmouth, New Hampshire poetry hoots. She has featured at local and regional events. She is in Alfred Nicol's ongoing workshop and Rhina Espaillat's lyceum classes. She has had a glass bead-making/jewelry business for 20 years and also draws and paints.

Michael Todd Steffen's first book, *Partner, Orchard, Day Moon,* was published in April 2014 by Cervena Barva Press. His poems and articles have appeared in a variety of locations, including *The Boston Globe, Connecticut Review, Poem* (Huntsville), *Taos Journal, Poetry Porch, Ibbetson Street* and in the window of the Grolier Poetry Bookshop.

Bert Stern writes in his home on Union Square. His third book, *What I Got for a dollar,* was launched on May 18, 2018.

Sandra Thaxter lives in Newburyport, Massachusetts. Born in Portland, Maine, she continues to spend summers on an island in Maine. She has studied poetry and writing in New York City at the Poetry Project at St. Marks, at the 92nd street Y. Currently she is studying with Alfred Nicol, and Rhina Espaillat of the Powow poets in Neewburyport. She has attended the Frost Farm spring poetry conference. Her academic background was in languages and comparative literature. She runs a non-profit and engages in social justice work.

Keith Tornheim, a biochemistry professor at Boston University School of Medicine, has five recent books, *I Am Lilith, Dancer on the Wind*; *Spirit Boat: Poems of Crossing Over*; *Can You Say Kaddish for the Living?*, *Fireflies*, and *Spoiled Fruit: Adam and Eve in Eden and Beyond.* His poems have appeared in *Ibbetson Street, The Somerville Times, Boston Literary Magazine, Muddy River Poetry Review* and *Poetica.*

Paulette Demers Turco is a student of Rhina Espaillat's annual Lyceum courses, Alfred Nicol's Poetry workshop in Newburyport, Massachusetts, and, for an MFA in Poetry, at Lesley University, where she received the MFA in writing President's Award. Her poetry is in *The Lyric, Ibbetson Street, Merrimac Mic Anthologies II, III,* and *IV*, and her first chapbook, *In Silence*, published by Finishing Line Press, June 2018 (www.finishinglinepress.com/product/in-silence-by-paulette-turco).

Elizabeth S. Wolf writes because stories are how we make sense of our world. Elizabeth's poetry appears in anthologies (*Persian Sugar in English Tea*, in English and Farsi; *Amherst Storybook Project*; *Mosaics: A Collection of Independent Women*; *The Best of Kindness*: Origami Poems Project) and journals *(New Verse News; Scarlet Leaf Review; Peregrine Journal)*. Her chapbook *What I Learned: Poems* was published by Finishing Line Press in 2017.

Sandra Wylie has been writing poetry for the last seven years. She was inspired by two great woman poets, Emily Dickenson and Anne Sexton. She also enjoys nature and photography. She used to be a pre-school teacher, and is now married and has two grown adult sons. She has been published in *Lucidity Poetry Journal, International* and has self-published many books, which are available on Amazon.